GEORGIA PETERKIN

WHAT *I TELL* MYSELF

DAILY EMOTIONAL, MENTAL & SPIRITUAL MOTIVATIONS AND MANTRAS

VOL I

WHAT I TELL MYSELF

Cover Design:

Interior Formatting: Nonon Tech & Design

Available on Amazon.

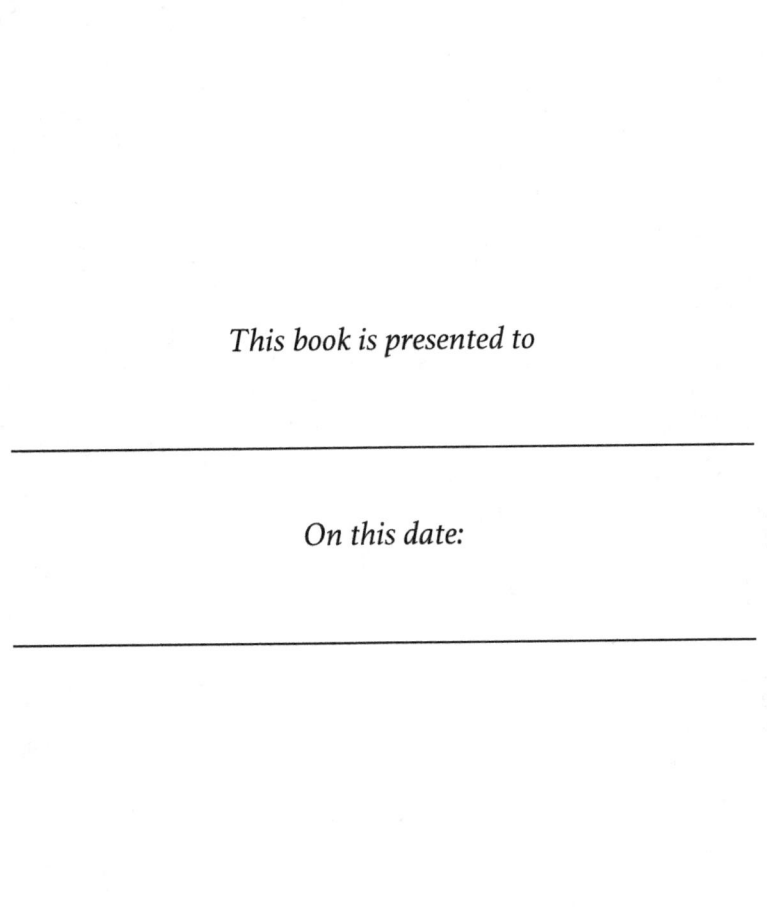

This book is presented to

_____

On this date:

_____

ACKNOWLEDGMENTS

First, I acknowledge God for being God, creating the universe, and making me a part of it. I believe the Universe is unfolding the way it should. I have the right to be here because God predestined this present moment for me to be here to write this book.

I thank Mr. William Marlin, Former Prime Minister of Dutch St. Maarten, one of the very first people who inspired and encouraged me to write this book based on the words of motivation I sent out every day for over six years.

I also acknowledge Mrs. Shahaira Richardson-Rey, a former banker; a phenomenal woman who often brings me to tears with her encouragement and acknowledgment.

For instance, when I had doubts, I read the random messages she sends to me, and all doubt would fly through the window, and I would be ready to do what I loved again. Shahaira is one of those people who makes you want to do better and be better at holding yourself accountable for your actions. She sees the good and calls out the very best in me.

To Teacher Trudyann Tomlin, who calls me her "WhatsApp Evangelist", I cannot tell you how often I would get a voice or text message from her saying, "You have a gift, you are talented, you need to write." You are such an inspiration to many with what you are doing. God is pleased with you. Thank you.

To my three wonderful children, Jovain D. Smith, Shaun-Taigh G. Lewis, and Naomie-Therese K. Soumarey; you are the reason I do what I do. For you all, I thrive to leave a legacy that cannot expire or be demolished, wealth that will be remembered and inherited by you all, your children, and the generations to come.

To "E," whose number I had on my phone, but did not know who he was (I use a pseudonym here to protect his privacy). However, I added him to my devotion podcast. About two years later, I received a text from him saying, "Thank you sis, you have made a difference in my life." Another eight months later, he said, "Since you started sending me these messages every day, I have learned to read, I have learned and understood a lot, so I want to tell you, don't stop." I must have read his message twenty times that day, as I cried. He explained that he went on the internet and looked up the words he did not understand. These are the moments I live for.

Then, to all those who have mistreated me, hurt me, betrayed me, lied about me, lied to me, defrauded me in business; overlooked and rejected me; and abused me even when I was a child... a resounding THANK YOU! A lot of content in this book was birthed because of how you made me feel; the thoughts you made me think; and the soul-searching I did while processing all the experiences. So, I truly and sincerely thank you! I often look through myself, and those "navel-gazing" moments are deep. Again, THANK YOU!

And finally, but most definitely not the least, I thank myself, my personality, my character, and my imperfect perfection. I thank all of me...

I LOVE YOU,
Georgia/ Gee/Gigi.

FOREWORD

I met Ms. Georgia Peterkin, affectionately known to most as Sis. Georgia, at a Women's Networking Fellowship meeting back in 2015, where Christian women come together to encourage, build up, and assist each other, regardless of the church they attend.

Her presence was captivating. She walked with a sense of grace and elegance. She's well- spoken and very well-kept; a true representation of a woman of God. When you see Sis Georgia, you will know she is a child of the Most High God.

However, it was not just her outer appearance that was captivating; it was her straightforward approach. I always felt compelled to tell Sis Georgia how refreshing it was to have met someone like her in the Kingdom; who when faced with conflict, addresses it immediately and settles the matter as soon as possible. Also, she does it with a soft but firm tone; so, you know she was hurt, yet gently enough for reconciliation to come out of that conversation.

Her love for God was easy for me to see, and I found it to be her greatest asset. It was because of her love for God that she would, in what I can only describe as a conscious decision, encourage others and spread the Word of God regardless of how she felt, and what she was going through at the time. Rejection never stopped her, even if it crossed her mind. I felt that spirit of perseverance whenever she was around.

I'm honored to know this woman of God and grateful that my obedience to the Holy Spirit to send Sis. Georgia an encouraging message out of the blue, was appreciated and heartfelt.

Now, she has taken all that love for God and people a step further to extend wisdom, love, knowledge, and encouragement to the world.

Anyone who reads this book will be glad they did.

I find this book, which represents principles and good character, instrumental in helping one live a productive life. It inspires and explains that we should not fear failure, but rather learn from it and press on. In a nutshell, it teaches one to practice the life Christ intended for us to live; as conquerors.

Sis Georgia, now known as Pastor Georgia, may God

continuously guide you and keep you covered. Stay focused and continuously allow God to move through you. To the readers; you have made one of your best decisions in choosing this motivational book.

—*Shahaira Richardson-Rey*

FOREWORD

I want to say that I am proud of you, Sis. Georgia Peterkin. I feel happy and fulfilled to see that you have taken your writing to a deeper level, where it's not confined to one platform; but has unlimited possibilities to reach all parts of the world. You are inspirational, a motivator, and an evangelist for the ones you love. You never get weary of posting the love of God to families and friends daily. You are faithful and committed indeed. You are my "WhatsApp Evangelist."

As a flower, I decree you will blossom. As a messenger of the Most High, you will go forth unfailingly, and as a light in a dark world, you will glow. As a counselor, you will touch the heart and lives of many. May success and progress find you and be the bed where you rest. May your divine destiny and purpose be your driving fuel. Continue to do what you are doing; as the Lord will grace you to do more.

It is with great pleasure that I recommend this book, to be read by families, couples, youths and adults—just about everyone. This book is a driving force for motivating and enlightening the soul and spirit. It contains principles drawn from God's word, which will effectively guide one in their day-to-day decision-making, as we venture through the journey called life.

It contains encouragement and words of wisdom that will mentor the mind and promote love and forgiveness. This book is a sword against all bitterness, self-defeating thought patterns, and negativity. May your soul be blessed as you journey through the pages of this book. You will be motivated for sure.

—*Teacher Trudyann Tomlin*

FOREWORD

I met this remarkable young lady at a book signing event. I was immediately captivated by how she treated everyone she interacted with, with a pleasant smile and a lot of grace. She is one of those rare people you meet who gives you no choice but to respect and admire her character. Georgia (Gigi) is strong yet polite and gentle. It doesn't matter who you are or what your social status is, she can affect you tremendously in a positive way. Receiving her daily quotes (devotionals) was always impactful. Many times, during my daily encounters, I would remember what she sent and put it into practice.

So, learning that she was compiling them to make a book was no surprise, as I was the one who kept on telling her that she should write one.

I am pleased to recommend this book to any and every one. This is the kind of book that belongs in every single household. It can and will benefit the young, the not-so-young, and the young at heart. Happy Reading.

—**William G. Marlin**
Former Prime Minister Dutch St. Maarten

THE AUTHOR'S
SHORT MEMOIR

Allow me to be vulnerable as I help you understand why *WHAT I TELL MYSELF* was paramount to how I overcame traumas, and how it made me the resilient, forgiving, soft, yet strong woman I am today.

As the fourth of ten children, life on Bowers Drive, Jamaica, was at the time, according to my understanding, "normal." We had a somewhat good life, my dad worked while my mom was mostly home taking care of the family. We ate well. Though we preferred when Dad cooked, as our plates would have more food on them. We had fun as children doing what children do. My dad (Papa Sonny) cultivated vegetables, fruits, and staples. He also raised chickens, pigs, and fish in our pond. He sold some of what he grew and of course, fed the family from it.

We looked forward to Sunday evenings, because there was always lots of food. Papa Sonny's friends would normally come to visit from the city. It was always a fun time, except when it was time to wash all those dishes.

Sunday also meant ice cream and Jell-O for us. Sundays were the best days.

However, there was another side to that life. My mom didn't physically hit us, but her words did. Dad, on the other hand, flogged us on schedule. We would line up every Saturday morning for our flogging; after Mom relayed all we did wrong throughout the week on Friday night. I was the one who was most afraid of getting spanked. It became a joke for the rest of my siblings, because the moment my name was called — meaning I was next for spanking — the pee would start running down my thighs.

In my later years, I started to understand why my mom was verbally abusive to us. She was under a lot of pressure. She was brought up in an abusive home and didn't know love. Then she was in a marriage with a man (my dad) who physically abused her. I suppose we were her outlet for her frustrations. I can honestly say she was really abused by my dad. But when there was no abuse, we were a happy family.

As a child not more than eight years old, while my mom was being physically abused by my father, I was being sexually abused by the son of a family friend. His name was Ken. He was about twenty-three or more. Families who lived in the country helped each other. So, sometimes, Ken and his mom, Mrs. Doris, would come over to our house and Mom might ask for something she needed. Ken would readily reply, *"Send di likkle renkin gyal fi it."* (Send the little feisty girl for it), meaning me. What Mom and no one else knew was that, every time I went over to his house and his mom wasn't there, he would lock the door, put me on the bed, and put his private parts between my legs, or on my genital area until he ejaculated. Then he would wipe me off, and threatened, "If I told anyone I would get flogged." So, of course, by now you understand I was afraid of being flogged; so, I told no one. However, every time I was sent over there, I walked as slowly as possible, stopping and looking back, hoping someone would see the fear in my eyes and not send me. But they only thought I was being stubborn and lazy. I guess my mom and dad were not educated about abuse and what to look for, or what questions to ask a child. Because I was never asked if anyone touched me inappropriately! It was a mistake I vowed not to make with my children, maybe I would even be overprotective because of my own childhood experiences.

As I got a bit older, perhaps ten to eleven years, it got worse when we visited our paternal grandfather. His yard housed many fruit trees, so it was a pleasure to visit. Sometimes, our parents would send us to visit him for one reason or the other. Then one horrible day, my granddad did the same thing that Ken was doing to me. I didn't understand what was going on, I thought it was normal. But I just didn't understand why I was always being told not to say anything or else I would get spanked. Then I started detesting going to my grandfather's house, but didn't dare say so to my parents because I would get what I was afraid of (beatings). I think it stopped when my grandfather died.

One time, my mom traveled to Europe, and we were left alone with our dad. Things went well, as much as I can remember. We might have gotten fewer beatings and more food! We also started getting some fancy clothing because Mom was sending them from Europe. I didn't go over to Mrs. Doris and Ken's house as often during that time either because Dad did not have the habit of asking them for anything or sending us to anybody's house, except family. One thing my parents made sure of was that we went to Sunday school. We all had to be in church every Sunday. I am grateful because this was how God planted his seed in me while the enemy was sowing destructive seeds of abuse in me.

After a few years, Mom returned to Jamaica, and of

course, back to the vicious cycle of abuse. There were times I watched her cry as my dad beat her. She never ever fought back!

Today, I still don't understand her reason for not fighting back, because she was not an easy nut to crack. I remember, once, while he was beating my mom, I took a broom and started hitting him, telling him to leave my mother alone. He gave me the look that said, "You will be next." So, I stopped and watched him continue beating her. I now understand that from a tender age, GEORGIA was being forged for a purpose through unpleasant experiences, or maybe I should say the enemy wanted to destroy me mentally and emotionally when I was a child, but God turned it around for my good as an adult.

There was a primary school exam called Common Entrance which all grade six students took. As it got closer to the exam, I remember my dad told me if I did not pass my exam, he would pay someone to kill me.

But at the same time, he sabotaged my efforts by not equipping me with what I needed for the exam. By the time the results were out, my dad had migrated to the United States. I passed but could not even attend the high school my passing grade qualified me for, due to financial challenges. I ended up in a school that was vastly lower in academic standards. My dad sent me a bracelet as a gift when I passed my common entrance exam.

There I was, starting a new school, and there was nothing new about me, except my shoes and books. But I really didn't care. I was more disappointed that I was not attending Glenmuir High School, which was the school my exam results qualified me to attend.. Dad had recently settled in the USA, so the finances weren't available, and so there was a lot of scarcity. Our mom did the best she could.

I was known to be feisty. My mouth was always ready to "tell you off," blackmail my siblings for food because I was the talker, and negotiate my way out of, or into whatever was necessary. This made me a businesswoman and a little bully, yet I had this big heart full of compassion. I remember planting my own little garden with callaloo (similar to spinach), and when it was ready, I would sell it for fifty cents per bundle. Most of the earnings would go to my mother, she would always borrow and say she would pay me back but never did. I did not mind because I took pride in knowing I could lend her money. After all, I was a businesswoman. I counted every single plant before

I went to school and counted them when I returned home. No one had the right to enter my garden without my permission.

There was a time I used to hide my money behind the refrigerator. One day, after I came home from school, my mom told me she wanted a loan. As usual, it was my moment to feel important by being asked for a loan. I headed towards the refrigerator to get the container with the money, but before I could retrieve it, she said, "I took it already." I suddenly had a fit! I cried and threw myself on the ground screaming, "I want my money! I want back my money!" I was robbed of my "moment of joy." That did not sit well with my mother, so I got a spanking for misbehaving. Another day, after counting my callaloo before school, I came back and counted and was missing a whole bundle, which was like six or seven stalks. I did what I did best. I threw myself on the ground and cried, kicked, screamed, and then uprooted every single one of those callaloo out of anger. What followed was a good scolding from my mother.

I did like giving to others, but dislike when what is mine is taken without my permission. Till date, I am that way. I would give you my all if you asked, but do not take what is mine without my permission.

Life Took a Turn for the Worse

In my first year at high school, hell broke loose for me and my siblings. We were already struggling because our father was away and I suppose he couldn't get a job. Our mother could only do so much in her power and will to support us. We walked a little over a mile to get to school. However, it was fun because we walked in groups and did all the foolish things you expect children on their way to and from school would. As I said, it was fun, even when the sun was hot! On one of such days, I was already halfway home when another child from my community came towards me from the opposite direction and yelled out my full name, as we all did when we wanted to make a statement... "Georgia Peterkin, yu nuh have nu house fi live inna!" (Georgia Peterkin, you don't have any house to live in). Me being the "feisty little girl" growing into a teenager now, I lashed out, "Shut yu stinkin moute" (Shut your stinking mouth); as I charged toward her ready to fight her. After all, the sun was hot; I had to walk more than one mile and was hungry too! She ran away from me because they all knew me to be a fighter. I continued on my way home with the taste of food already on my tongue because of how hungry I was.

As I approached my home, it seemed like a crowd

gathered at my gate, but wasn't sure... I started running to get there. When I got close enough, to my surprise, that little chatty-mouthed girl from my community was right! There was no house, our furniture was on the street along with the rest of my siblings, with crowd from the community gathered around. By then, our mom had not been with us for over two weeks, because she had mysteriously fallen ill and could not even stay at home. So, our good neighbor, Mr. Reid, watched over us. The land my parents built on was under a lease and sale agreement, and they lived there for decades. The owners, however, were ill-mannered people, which everyone in the community knew. The rumors were that they did witchcraft on my mom so they could be free to do what they wanted since my dad was no longer around, and they were very afraid of my dad and my mom.

After being surprised by such devastation and the reality of being homeless, I grabbed a machete and started running down the road with tears streaming down my face with the intention of going to the Campbel's house; I was determined to take revenge. I don't remember the details, but I knew adults were running after me. Eventually, they stopped me, held me, and disarmed me. As the night went on, Mr. Reid decided that he had to take responsibility for Joyo's children (Joyo is the name he gave my mom instead of calling her Joy). The adults around helped to take our furniture to Mr. Reid's house. He had a very big house like a two-family home, so he placed us in the smaller half of the house. Still, weeks went by and there was no news of our mom. Life became a nightmare for me and my siblings. Even though Mr. Reid was nice, we had lost our home; we didn't know where our mom was, and dad did not have his permit to work in the USA yet and couldn't risk leaving. Attending school became a rarity, thus we were lost.

Joy's Voice

About two months after the ordeal of our losing our home, we were in bed one night when we heard voices (that of a male and a female). When my siblings and I listened carefully, to our surprise, it was Joy's voice. Our mother! We all jumped out of the bed and raced towards the door shouting, "Joy! Joy! Joy!" We were happy to see our mother. The last time I remember seeing her before her disappearance, she did not look like my mom; she looked like a "scary person from a movie," and then disappeared. We later found out that it was Mr. Reid who had taken her to a "spiritual person's" residence to stay, while he "worked" on her. When we ran to her from our room, she was smiling, and we recognized her as the mom we'd always known. She held us all as if her arms were long enough to embrace eight of us all at once.

We didn't ask any questions because that was not our upbringing. We never questioned adults! Our mom told us to get back to our room, which we reluctantly did, but we were all happy that she was back. We hardly slept that night as we tried very hard to hear what she and Mr. Reid were discussing. As usual, these two neighbors could talk for hours. We often got impatient when they met each other at the fence that separated our land, because that meant dinner would be late! (I was always a food lover along with my brothers, Bobby and Ronald).

We woke up the next morning and our mom was still with us. She made us breakfast and sent us off to school. And when we came home that evening, Joy was gone! We were crushed all over again. We stayed with Mr. Reid for about six months, with no news from or about our mother. Though Mr. Reid kept on saying, "*Joyo alright unu soon hear from har* (Joy is okay, you will all soon hear from her)." I didn't know if he was in contact with her, or he was just trying to comfort us.

Eventually, we rented a house with the help of Mr. Reid, and moved there. It was on the same street as our paternal relatives, so that was cool! We had a lot of cousins, and we were all close growing up. Our older brother and sister became the "father and mother." My brother was seventeen years old and my sister was sixteen. The youngest brother was less than one year old. We had each other, and we were happy to be together. School became a struggle. My older brother, Greg, my older sister Marci, and I, were all brilliant in school, earning straight As. However, we were not allowed to attend school as often as we liked. My older brother got a job at a juice factory, and that was what sustained us for a while. I will forever love him... He took a lot of blame for us. He was soft, but when it came to us, he was a beast! He would protect and defend us and cry at the same time.

By then, our older sister was trying to make her own life. She entered several beauty competitions and won. She represented our parish and the country in different cultural and national beauty pageants. This was also somewhat of a win for us because she contributed to our well-being. We were all living alone, looking out for and after each other, and we were fine....

Our Grandmother Appeared

Eventually, our mother became active in our lives again. She thought that we needed an adult around, which was true seeing that we were all still young. So, my mom decided our grandmother (her mom) was the best person to look after us. In a normal family, that would be true. In our case, we were entering a period of unimaginable hunger, neglect, and abuse. By this time, I was thirteen or fourteen years.

In the first weeks of her arrival, everything seemed to be going well, but as time progressed, we saw that Tanisha, our maternal cousin whom our grandmother brought with her to live with us, was being favored; getting more attention and more things from granny. Food became even scarcer for us. Granny was always saying there was nothing to eat, because Joy, (our mother) or Sonny, (our father) didn't send anything for us. However, Tanisha was always getting money and food from her. And if we asked her to share with us, Granny quarreled with us, telling us to leave her alone. Tanisha was a darling, she never really listened to Granny. She found ways to hide food and share with us anyway.

Things really went from bad to worse, no school, no food, and no money—a deplorable way to live.

Of course, by then, Mom and Dad were in the "battle of the sexes." There were pay phones so we could call them from time to time. There was a lady few houses down the road who had a home phone. Our Dad would call us there at specific times, so we were able to call our parents from time to time. When we called them, we would ask for things. For example, if we called our mom and asked her for money to buy something or to go to school, she would say, "Ask your father," and when we called our father and asked him for money, he would say, "Ask your mother, I don't have money." So, they were in a war with each other and we were caught in the crossfire as innocent children.

However, one good thing we realized was that our dad sent several barrels to us from time to time. When he sent the barrels, it would be three or four barrels of food and clothes at the same time. There was a period when we were getting "stuff" from our father. However, when they arrived; the benefits were limited due to the fact that, three-quarter of what was in the barrels would go to our grandmother's children in the city. They were all grown adults with the youngest being twenty-two years old. They would come every weekend, and she would fill their bags with groceries and other items. We were not allowed to take anything from the barrels.

However, we would hide and take stuff whenever we were hungry. We would, well let's say, "steal," what was ours in the first place.

Our mom was sending money, we just didn't know because our grandmother always said there was no money for food, or to go to school. One day, Nicky (my sister) and I decided to play "hide and seek" to forget about our hunger; so, she hid under the bed. The base of the bed was springs. As she lay flat on her back under the bed looking up, right in front of her eyes was a coil of USD bills! It was the money our grandmother received from our mother and was hiding from us. Nicky, my sister and "partner in crime" (my grandmother never liked to see us together, because she knew that spelled trouble for the rest of the day) took a few of the USD bills and we left! We had hit the jackpot! We ate well that day.

At that time, our paternal grandmother was living on the same street, a little way down from where our house was. She is one of the sweetest grandmothers I have ever met. She wears her heart on her sleeve. Every time she gave us something, she would tell us, "It's the last I have, no more," until another cousin went to see her. Then she repeated the same thing. "Barry G," as everyone called her, did her best to help us. To this day,

I don't understand why we were not left in her care. Oftentimes, when she saw us coming, she would cry, and always find something to give us and still have enough to give the other grandchildren. There were many! Hunger was no little thing for us.

One summer holiday after I had to drop out of school, my aunt decided she was going to take me to Kingston City with her. I was happy! How was I supposed to know that I was about to experience sexual abuse all over again?

I arrived in Kingston with my aunt, and everything seemed fine, my other aunts and my uncle were all nice. But I noticed quite soon that when all my aunts left for work, my uncle would always find something new to give me, like shorts, little tops, etc. then he would tell me to put them on so he could see if they fit. I complied. He soon started making sexual advances towards me, telling me to come and lay beside him. However, during this time, I was the maid in the house. I was in charge of tidying the house, cooking, sweeping the yard, filling the drum with water while everyone was at work, and babysitting my aunt's little son. But I didn't mind doing all of that, because I loved my aunts. Moreover, they gave me nice clothes to wear, and I was always a fashionista.

My uncle abused me both sexually and physically. He would hit me all the time. I remember when he had gotten a girl pregnant, and she ended up staying in the country with my grandmother and siblings. I was punished for telling my mom which I didn't do. My uncle kicked me in the back of my knee, while my back was turned! I cried for hours because I knew I didn't do it. I did not know that his baby's mother was in the country. The kick was very hard. My aunt came home, and I told her. This caused a huge quarrel between them. However, the sexual and physical abuse continued, and I remained silent.

By then, I had friends, Misty, Theresa, and my boyfriend, Devon. Yes, he was my boyfriend because I liked him, and he liked me because all we did when we saw each other was laugh. It was a pleasure to get water because the pipe was close to Devon's house and I had a chance to see him.

There was a church right behind my grandmother's house where I lived with my aunt. People always had the worst things to say about the Pastor. There came a time when the church was hosting a crusade on the church's large ground. Misty, Theresa, and I decided to go over to the church that night, not to attend church but to meet up with other friends including Devon.

I couldn't wait for the night to come. We were going to have the time of our life in that churchyard while the crusade was going on.

When the night finally came, we went over, and the church crusade was in full swing, but so were our plans to have fun. Devon arrived and I was on top of the world even though we were not talking; we were just being "extra "in front of each other, but that was enough. Eventually, I was at the church window at the entrance of the church, looking out and laughing at what was going on because they were speaking a different language that I thought was funny.

I cannot tell what happened after that, but I regained consciousness at the altar in front of the entire church with people clapping, while some were shouting and speaking in that strange language. I was completely confused about what was happening. More importantly, I didn't know how I got there. I was looking around to see where my friends were... Devon! Did Devon see the charade? No! I hoped he didn't. I wanted to just shrink to the earth out of embarrassment. They told me I was filled with the Holy Spirit and speaking in the same language I was laughing at.

That night, I went home feeling both embarrassed and

joyful. The next day, I told my aunts what happened, but they took it lightly. I was impatient for the night to come, not because I wanted to see my friends and Devon like the night before, but because of my curiosity to see what would happen. I went on a crusade that evening but this time, I did not stay outside, I sat at the back. For the first time in my life, I was feeling something that I couldn't understand but loved. I was about fifteen years old at the time. I started going to the church, and in my first week of attendance, they signed me up for a Bible quiz with the other teenagers of the church. Hence, the very first book of the Bible I studied and knew by heart was the book of Ruth because we were going to be quizzed on that. Within two weeks being filled with the Holy Spirit, I was baptized! A NEW CREATURE! OLD THINGS PASS AWAY, ALL THINGS BECOME NEW.

I suddenly started defying my uncle's sexual and physical abuse... I really don't know how, but it just started happening. So, he stopped.

I wanted to go back to school; I was still a teenager and wanted a normal teenage life. I was intelligent and ambitious, but had no direction. Soon enough, I started spending more and more time with church sisters my age, I spent time at their houses and at one point even lived with one of them. The problem was: they were in school, and I wasn't. I was still loving the newfound relationship I had with God through the Holy Spirit.

I was sent back to the country, and I continued going to church. There was a church right across our house that we used to attend.

Life was hard as usual; I came back to the same treatment from my maternal grandmother; nothing had changed. So, I decided I was going to effect change for myself and my siblings. I got a job in the city, which involved living there and looking after a little girl. It was just her and her mother; the job was okay. There was a boy and a girl my age who were neighbors, so we blended well and did teenage stuff. I was earning sixty dollars every week, and no one was prouder than I was. I was able to go home on some weekends and shop for my siblings. I had that same proud feeling as I did with my callaloo garden. Eventually, that lady lost her job and could no longer pay for a live-in babysitter, so I also lost my job. When I went back home again, I decided I wanted to continue schooling. I enrolled myself in a school, sat for the entrance exam, passed with an above-average mark, and was happy that I was going back to school. However, when I called my parents to let them know I needed money for registration, uniforms, and other supplies, my mother told me to ask my father, and he told me to ask my mother. I was yet again denied the opportunity to further my education.

Moving Around in Search of Security

Once again, I went back to the city, but, this time, with another aunty who was well off. I was expected to be the maid, but I had food and a sense of security. She decided to let me go back to school because I was very determined and intelligent. I was a talker, too! I got enrolled in a Community College, did the exam, passed, and was ready for school. I was so excited! But, as fate would have it, my dad flew back from the USA. My aunt then thought it was reasonable for him to contribute to my school supplies. I went down the country to meet my dad and told him the good news, and what my aunt said. I was heartbroken when my dad told me he had no money for that. What was worse, was having to relay that message to my aunt. And just like that, everything fell apart including my hope, dream, and excitement to return to school. My aunt thought and said, if my dad didn't want to help me, then why should she? I thought, who could blame her? She was right. I continued living with her until it became unbearable, I could no longer take her slave-like treatment and verbal abuse, and she was always threatening to send me back to what she considered the "rat hole." So, I went back! In my quest to find a place of security, comfort, and hope to be able to help my siblings, I suffered attempted sexual abuse from other male family members and strangers alike. I suffered rejection, wrong accusations, hatred, mistreatment, and abandonment.

I can't remember crying because of those traumas. In fact, I knew they were bad things, but did not know how to identify all those experiences or what to call them. I was always resilient, always focused on coming up with a plan. By then I had stopped going to church and filled that void with other things. This included relationships forged through the quest for finding love, acceptance, stability, and security. But I found physical abuse instead. I was never the one to take a hit, so I always fought back and fought back hard.

This was just a window for you, my readers; to see through and understand why motivation and mantras are so dear to me. From very early in my life, I kept saying to myself; "it will get better and I will not always be living like this. When I get older, I will change my life." I had no idea I was already planting positive seeds in my own life. Looking back, I often wonder how I managed to remain compassionate and caring with a very pure heart!

As an adult, the only thing I did not experience, which I experienced in my childhood, was sexual abuse. And what's more, the most devastatingly painful experience I had as an adult came from church folks, and people that I loved, and thought were my friends, and thought I could trust. The level of ungratefulness, lies, and betrayal coming from them was surreal! This is when I started journaling my feelings and thoughts through quotes and mantras. I observed the way people treated and communicated with each other, sometimes rather poorly and with disregard for the feelings of other people.

When I was angry, hurt, frustrated, scared, uncertain, and confused, I entered my thoughts and put them into words. Then I started sharing devotions to encourage others, using many from what I journaled.

My intention is to write a complete memoir of my life and experiences, since this hasn't even scratched the surface.

WHAT I TELL MYSELF is what got me through and still does today.

WHAT I TELL MYSELF

"DAILY EMOTIONAL, MENTAL, AND SPIRITUAL
MOTIVATIONS, AND MANTRAS"

1.   I am strong, I am courageous, I am capable, and I
     am not afraid. I can do everything I commit to and
     put my mind into, through Christ who gives me
     the strength. I am not perfect, but I am enough.
     I may not be the best, but I am certainly not the
     worst. Everything will be okay, I will get better,
     and I am getting better.

2.   All it takes is belief. If you believe completely in
     something or someone, you will never give up on
     it, even when you don't feel like it. But you must
     know and believe it is worth fighting for.

3.   Giving up on what does not show signs of progress
     or a fulfilling future does not make you weak; it
     speaks of responsible choices and strength.

4. Speaking with integrity is better than getting carried away with your emotions. Conduct your life with integrity, not emotions.

5. Failure or frustration cannot define your life unless you allow it.

6. Be happy right where you are; don't wait for a special event or person to be happy. You'll miss out on experiencing all that joy and happiness that's already waiting inside of you.

7. There's no true authority that does not come with responsibility. So, if you want authority, show responsibility.

8. You can fall on the rock and be broken, or the rock will fall on you and crush you to dust (it's in your best interest to fall on the rock).

9. Do not accept being "tolerated." Make sure that, wherever you are, with whoever you're around, whatever you're doing, you are, ACCEPTED, APPRECIATED, and RESPECTED.

10. Let your work, not your words, speak for you.

11. You have the privilege and choice to place yourself wherever you choose to. If you place yourself among the great thinkers, and the wise movers and shakers, you will become all of that. If you place yourself among mediocre and low-level thinkers and achievers, that is what you will become.

12. To maintain authenticity and integrity, you MUST be prepared to stand out, be "ODD," and be at odds with the masses.

13. After fulfilling the precepts of God, fulfill your principle and value, not anyone else's.

14. None of us are invincible, but some of us are irreplaceable.

15. Pride will allow you not to admit it, but time will prove the truth about it.

16. Lions don't have to roar to be feared; their presence is enough (Sometimes, silence speaks louder than words).

17. The workers are not always the talkers; the talkers are not always the workers. Not everyone making noise or sound is actually doing something or making an impact.

18. Measure your effort by your result. Focus your time and energy on mastering and executing a plan (Your plan).

19. It is okay to love yourself, just don't idolize yourself.

20. Avoid the energy-draining practice of telling people what you are doing. Instead, spend your time and effort doing the necessary things to accomplish a successful result that will explain itself. (All will see; great results cannot be hidden).

21. My power is not to make me important but to empower others.

22. You are not powerful until you've empowered someone else.

23. It's okay to seek for yourself, but think about others in the process.

24. In the book of Ruth, the reapers were told by Boaz to leave something for Ruth to glean for herself. Moral: Just because you can take all, doesn't mean you should. Those without possibility still need equal opportunity.

25. You don't need to be friends with someone to help them. In fact, you don't even need to like them, but you must be full of the agape that is accompanied by compassion and will cause you to help them.

26. Being wise doesn't mean I know everything. It means I am cautious when I listen and even more cautious when I speak.

27. In speaking, know everything you say, but never say everything you know.

28. Eating your own words is better than someone making you swallow them.

29. A fool can never pretend to be wise, but a wise person knows how to pretend to be a fool.

30. There are four vital things to look for in a person, especially those in your circle: Truth, Love,

Honesty, and Integrity. If they lack the last one, there is a good chance they do not have the others.

31. True love towards each other will never produce envy, jealousy, grudges, unforgiveness, or hate.

32. Mouth or self-recognition love will never allow you go the extra mile for someone. You do so only when you love deeply, from the base of your heart.

33. No matter what man in his strength does or says, he will never prevail against the Holy God.

34. Before every victory, there is always a test, and every level produces new challenges.

35. I was made for this; I might bend, but I will never break.

36. Three things are hard to do or not do but necessary for mental, emotional, and even spiritual growth: Don't worry, don't react, and don't take revenge.

37. Certain things are designed to teach us what to think, not how "to think" (Mind colonization).

38. If you keep looking at yourself, you will not see others. If you keep looking at others, you will not see yourself (Keep it balanced).

39. Some bad people in our lives must remain. You cannot get rid of them until their purpose has been accomplished.

40. You are not strong when you control others; you become strong when you can control "self."

41. You cannot be a success in the outside world and a failure in your home.

42. Your home is your training ground. Master your skills there, and you will be ready to take on the world.

43. The strategy might or can change, but the principle and the goal remain the same.

44. "Impression vs. Impact" (Impact lives; don't impress people).

45. Your calling, authority, and gifts are recognized by others even without you noticing.

46. Your life is a story; boldly write the script so the world can read it clearly enough.

47. Nothing about your experiences should be regretted. But everything should be noted for future reference.

48. Knowing what is right is a plus; doing what is right is a MUST.

49. Be "UP and OUT" about it. Learn to speak up and speak out about injustice, and act on your passion for change.

50. "THE CHALLENGE." Challenge yourself to challenge yourself to challenge yourself.

51. Look beyond the conventional idea of marriage, relationships, and friendships to find the part that appeals to you. Choose the parts you want to commit to and be loyal to. Build on it and make it your safe haven.

52. As long as you are uncomfortable where you are, it means that's not your final stop.

53. In-between vision and provision is preparation.

54. There is so much good in the worst of us, and so much bad in the best of us that it hardly behooves all of us to speak negatively about any of us.

55. I will not be in the middle of the ocean and allow soap to get in my eyes (wise proverb).

56. To succeed, you must find something to hold on to. You will need that as your mantra or anchor to motivate and steadily hold you when all seems unstable and uncertain.

57. Make commitments to yourself and keep to them, or you will never be able to make commitments to anything or anyone else and keep to them.

58. No action should be taken, and no words should be spoken without being thoroughly considered.

59. Key represents control, so whatever or whoever you hold the keys to, you have the power to control and vice versa.

60. It is said that "in giving, you will receive." This saying is true not only in your finances but also in encouragement, love, compassion, and respect.

— Georgia Peterkin

" Sometimes the "MESSAGE" is in what was NOT said, in what was said.

61. Sometimes, we look around or inside of us and feel hopeless, as though there's no end or solution in sight. Remember, the only time all hope is lost is when you stop hoping or stop breathing. Never give up.

62. The difference between being healed and being made whole is that you are touched in one area or the other, but being made whole is complete restoration—nothing missing, nothing lacking.

63. Truly, to protect your heart from being broken is to pretend you don't have a heart that can be broken, but in pretending, you cancel all possibilities of meeting or receiving from another heart that is filled with love and healing.

64. Keeping your hands closed will not allow anyone to take what you have. But it also prevents you from receiving more than what you have.

65. Standing alone and being recognized is better than standing in the crowd and being lost.

66. Learning the art of kindness takes practice. Practice on yourself (Be kind to yourself).

67. Knowledge has no power unless applied. It's not so much about what you know but what you do with what you know.

68. 6The longer the rain falls, the more the earth is soaked, and the more the earth is soaked, the moister it gets. Moral: The more time and energy you spend on whatever you want to achieve, the firmer and more durable your plan will be.

69. Being alone is different than being lonely.

70. An important aspect of disciplined autonomy is recognizing how your action affects others.

71. You can be forthright and not be brutal with your honesty.

72. Love is the bedrock on which everything that lasts is built.

73. The only real intervention comes from God. Intervene on my/our/their behalf now, Lord, Jehovah Gibbor.

74. Mastering your faith is knowing how to worship when times get hard.

75. Hard times will determine who or what you are loyal to.

76. The worst lies can be the ones you tell yourself.

77. Your loyalty to someone does not mean they will be loyal to you in return. You can only hope that love, integrity, and fairness abide in that person.

78. What if you give but never get anything back in return? Always remember that this can happen. But most importantly, remember that you can still choose to live your best life anyway.

79. There is a difference between healthy compromise and being taken advantage of. You should not always be the one who has to compromise.

80. If you have to censor everything about you (your laugh, what you say, your thoughts, even your personality, and character), you are in a very toxic place.

81. Do not move against yourself; that's a sure progress blocker.

82. You will not always be able to fix everything you want to fix. But you sure can forgive, let go, and move on.

83. Bad emotional residue from your past is the number one killer of potentially great relationships in your future.

84. Our realities might be different, but they all matter equally.

85. Teaching people "to think" is not the same as telling them "what" to think.

86. When there are no alternative facts, you will repeat the secondary truth.

87. It is your right as my sister/brother/fellow human to correct me if you are sure I am wrong or making a mistake. And it is my right and duty to stop, listen, and consider your correction before I move forward.

88. It is good to appreciate someone who is good for you and who does good things for you. But never worship that person. Worship the one who sent that person—GOD.

89. Your motive decides the weight and credibility of your action.

90. Knowledge is every human being's birthright, do not allow yourself to be robbed of it.

91. A relief soothes immediately but has a temporary effect. A cure takes a while but has lasting or permanent results.

92. Silence, sometimes, has the loudest voice to the person who understands that sound.

93. Sometimes, adding value to someone's life is subtracting yourself from it, and vice versa.

94. What God keeps is well-kept.

95. Find effective ways to pursue the things and people that will affect you positively.

96. Just because you've reached your limit doesn't mean you've reached the end. It just means that it is time for God to step in with his limitless capacity, power, and knowledge.

97. If the love you give isn't accepted, it's okay to feel it but not to continue giving it. (You can feel it, but you don't have to express it to the wrong person).

98. When you stop fighting the tide, you will start floating on the waves, and then you can plan your next stroke.

99. As long as you stand in the ant's nest, you will get bitten. Move and see what happens.

100. Progressiveness, sometimes, calls for aggressiveness.

101. Reactions are often impulsive, but Re-Action is calculative and intentional, whether good or bad (Change of action).

102. Makeup does not make an ugly heart beautiful. If you want to be beautiful, fix your character, attitude, and integrity.

103. Intelligence is so sexy and irresistible.

104. Faith is believing even when you think there is no reason to believe.

105. Sacrifice is not the same as stupidity. Recognize when you are being plain stupid in your devotion and sacrifice for someone.

106. Saying "NO" does not mean rejecting someone or having any ill feelings for them. It is okay to say "NO" without feeling guilty.

107. The best thing you can do for yourself sometimes is to say "NO."

108. Submission does not mean you should accept everything given or done to you. Learn to demand what you desire and what you are worth.

109. You will accomplish more when your heart and mind are aligned.

110. A person may never verbalize "I LOVE YOU." But for as long as you've known them, everything they've done to and for you; says, "I LOVE YOU."

111. It is better to see it than to hear it.

112. Integrity is better than popularity.

113. Criticism is not always bad; it is necessary and needed sometimes.

114. When it comes to people, you don't have to look very far to find trouble or those with bad intentions. But it's also true that you don't have to look very far to find peace or those with good intentions. (It's a matter of changing your perspective).

115. If there is just a little flicker, keep blowing, but make sure you see the flicker, or it will be wasted breath.

116. Your life is your storybook. Do not let anyone write on your pages without your consent. But most importantly, make sure what is written is what you want in your life story.

117. If you are reading this, that means you are still breathing, and if you are still breathing, that means you still have a chance to live, start over,

forgive, love and be loved, achieve, and be happy. Take that chance and go for it.

118. Passion is good but dangerous without wisdom and patience.

119. Wisdom is good; intelligence is also good. But it's better to use wisdom than intelligence when dealing with a foolish or simple-minded person.

120. Wisdom discerns what intelligence doesn't understand.

Daily Reminder

What a **DAY**
doesn't teach you,
the **YEARS** will.

@GeorgiaPeterkin

121. Even in the desert, you can still find beauty.

122. It's difficult to appreciate joy until you have fully tasted sadness. Laughter is sweeter if you have experienced tears.

123. An encouraging call or a sincere hug can be an oasis in someone's desert.

124. Everything that carries value in life is guarded by something or someone. You can never access value without overcoming the obstacle that is protecting it.

125. Growth and achievement in life require different things at different times. Sometimes you must isolate yourself like an eagle in molting, and other times you have to surround yourself with an alliance like a pride of lions.

126. I don't seek pity; I seek an opportunity because I was created to thrive, not pitied.

127. When you are at the top, you become a "topic." Everyone wants to know how you did... When you did... Where you did... Why you did... Your duty

is not to give answers but to continue to inspire others by remaining at the top.

128. A good glass of red wine, a good laugh, and some sleep are great remedy for stress.

129. Sometimes what you need to get ahead is what money cannot buy, such as a favor. When you receive what money cannot buy, you can use it to attract money.

130. Be careful not to go from being a helping hand in times of need to a constant source for every need.

131. Kindness can be easily taken for granted if you do not manage your kindness carefully. Some people will not stop eating candy until the jar is empty.

132. If you could see people's hearts reflected on their faces, even some you call friends would not be qualified to enter your space.

133. If God was going to do everything for humanity, He would not say, "By the sweat of your brow, you shall eat bread" (Gen 3:19), or "if you do not work,

you should not eat" (2 Thes 3:10). We have a God given role to play in making our lives better.

134. If you are proud, you will not get help. No one wants to help pride because pride knows not appreciation and gratitude.

135. When you give, do not give because it is convenient. Give because it is commanded and recommended.

136. Giving is not warfare; it is worship.

137. Every single person has something to give in this life. If not money, it's time. If not time, then love. If not love respect. If not respect, compassion. But we all have something to give.

138. True generosity is when those who can hardly afford to be generous still are.

139. If your emotion is on someone else's life support who does not care if you live or die, it is time to pull the plug. You will find that you can breathe. You were able to breathe all along but were stuck

with a bad connection and never gave yourself a chance.

140. We often say, "This person or that person is hurting me," but if truth be told, they are not hurting us. We are hurting ourselves. A person can only do what you allow them to do to you.

141. What you accept is what you will get. Good or bad, spiritual, or natural.

142. When you notice people are swerving in and out of your life lane, kindly ask them to get out of your lane—because they are obstructing traffic that can take you places they do not intend to take you.

143. When God is pleased with you, He will protect you—no need to seek other protection or defend yourself.

144. There are times when God will say to your storm, "Peace be still," and other times, He will say to your soul, "Be at peace, and ride out your storm, for I am with you."

145. When you are being pleased, whether by a person or a situation, it is easier for you to please another with pleasure and without measure.

146. Words are nice, but ACTIONS are exquisite.

147. The more humorous you are while working, the less stressed you will be, and you will be more productive and happier about what you do.

148. If your environment is not to your liking, be more liking to your environment.

149. Humor and intelligence make a great tag team.

150. Work can be more fun if you are funnier while you work.

151. Humor is pervasive and pleasantly intrusive.

152. Laugh at yourself. It makes you realize that you are great company and a self-entertainer.

153. If you are speaking to a crowd that makes you nervous, look in the crowd for the one or two

faces that agree with you. Then draw courage from them by making eye contact with them more frequently.

154. People who poke fun at themselves make others feel more comfortable; give them what they want. Be confident enough to make the craziest jokes about yourself and remain assertive and sure of yourself.

155. Humor is both laughing with and laughing at, laughing with others and laughing at yourself.

156. Humility is taking pride, ego, and arrogance and keeping them at bay so you can serve, lead, and inspire without motives.

157. A great universal combination is honesty, integrity, humility, and humor.

158. Whisper while you invent, work quietly, think carefully, and act wisely. In the end, you will have noise all around you—made by those who didn't know, didn't think, and didn't believe that you could or would.

159. Our safe place protects us, but it also keeps away possibilities and opportunities.

160. Be the kind of person that can move an entire room. Not by speaking, acting, or showing. But by simply "being." Let your very presence speak.

161. Human beings are the masters of self-deception. We fool ourselves into believing false things and refuse to believe things that are true.

162. We lie to ourselves because we do not have enough psychological strength to admit the truth and deal with the consequences that follow.

163. Your negative emotions are just as valid as your positive emotions. They are warning signs that you need to pay attention to a certain thing or person. Accept them but don't live by them.

164. We allow our thoughts to deceive us through polarized thinking or cognitive distortion— extreme thinking, emotional reasoning, or over- generalizing. Don't take one bad experience and use it as an infinite expectation.

165. Our lives are meaningless until we give them meaning.

166. Most of us are culturally deceived and are conditioned to live, think, act, and believe culturally rather than doing all the above by ourselves and with free will.

167. We sometimes accept things because we believe we are supposed to, and not because we think or believe it is right for us.

168. It is true words cannot break your bones, but they can certainly shatter your heart, your dreams, your self-confidence, your very being. Words can take every ounce of strength and courage from you. If you receive, accept, and hold on to these words.

169. We all use each other as a garbage disposal, and most of the time, the people closest to us become our garbage bins. We dump our bad and unwanted emotions on them (anger, fear, jealousy, frustration, insecurities, hate, unforgiveness, bad workday, etc.). Suppose the recipient does not know how to recycle what they have received. In

that case, they will store the garbage and end up with an emotionally polluted environment and a badly wounded self.

170. Fear can cause us to take up full residence in obscurity—afraid of what is out there on the other side of the light.

171. The unknown is a beautiful place when you have an awesome vision of it.

172. No rhythm, no movement, no movement, no sound, no sound, no life; they all intertwine.

173. The only opinions that should matter are God's and yours. No other opinion should be allowed to alter your God-given destiny.

174. When you start taking full responsibility for who you are, you will stop hurting yourself and others around you.

175. Confrontation, at times, is the only solution.

176. Acknowledging the many lies we tell ourselves is the beginning of being free from self-deception.

177. Every thought you have, every person you blame or accuse, every word spoken to justify you, take a pause, re-evaluate, and see if you find "you" in the center of all that.

178. Avoiding a situation or person is not finding the solution.

179. Confrontation does not have to be aggressive, argumentative, or violent. But it must be firm and resolute.

180. The walking "out of" is necessary for you to have the "walking into."

— Georgia Peterkin

"Maybe you're not **OVER** him/her. But you are definitely over that **toxic situation.**" Freedom road feels **LIBERATING** when it's what you've been **longing** for.

181. It is never about how much you are asking but who you are asking. If you ask for a dollar from someone who only has a dime, you are asking too much.

182. The person who is unprepared to or does not want to meet your demands or expectations, will always think that you are demanding too much, when in fact, they really have very little to offer YOU.

183. You will never conquer what you are afraid to challenge. Sometimes what you think is challenging is only in your mind and not reality.

184. The truth is, it is much better when we can acknowledge where we went wrong and say, "I am sorry." Too often, we allow pride to stop us from asking for forgiveness from those whom we have wronged. You feel so free when you say I am sorry or when you speak the truth instead of a lie, especially as sons and daughters of God.

185. I am not a liability in any relationship; I am an asset.

186. I am synchronized to the divine timing of God and will move in his timing.

187. People will misunderstand you and what is perspicuous to formulate accusations against you. Don't waste your energy and time on these folks. Dust them off and put them out of your mind, then move on with business/life like they don't exist, and never give them the pleasure of being angry or upset with them. They are to be pitied. They are lost, have lost, and are still losing.

188. "WE" is greater than "I." "US" is stronger than "ME." "OUR" is more powerful than "MY."

189. Sometimes, God breaks our spirit to save our soul; sometimes, He breaks our hearts to make us whole. Sometimes, God allows pain to make us stronger. Sometimes, God permits failure to make us humble. Sometimes, He allows illness so we can take better care of ourselves. Sometimes, He takes everything away so we can learn the value of what He gives us.

190. You should make plans but remember we live by God's grace. So, whatever you have or will accomplish, remind yourself that it is God's will, so trust His heart, even when you can't see His hands.

191. Tell yourself this: God LOVES ME with an everlasting love and PROMISED that He will not withhold any good thing from me if I call on Him.

192. Enjoying your children and God's CREATION is a luxury. You should thank God for every opportunity to see the goodness of life and for being a part of His goodness.

193. To give up my pleasure of being alone or single, your presence has to feel better and be better than my solitude. Freedom at any level is priceless.

194. When you secretly put or keep others down so you or yours can rise, that is not success; it is evil and wickedness. But there is a set time to expose and bring down every evil work, rise, and achievement. There is nothing in "dirty work" to be proud of or to be considered a success.

195. We all parade the ideology of "I would rather be hurt by the truth than to be thrilled with a lie." But, if truth be told, it is easier for the heart to believe a lie than for the brain to accept the truth.

196. Be willing to bleed for self-growth, self-recognition, self-worth, and self-acceptance. It sometimes comes with a painful price. You must be willing to become a temporary enemy to yourself to become self-disciplined for the sake of personal growth.

197. There are always growing options; you just need to water them, so they grow into choices and chances.

198. Many great and intelligent men and women fall victim to the eyes that lead to their destruction (Ask King Solomon, King David, and Samson).

199. Getting your heart and your brain to cooperate with each other is not always easy. They always fight against each other on matters of love, relationships, and decision-making. You must know which one is practical and in sync with reality.

200. The problem is not so much that you are not where you should be but that you do not practice being who you are right where you are.

201. Plan right where you are, but let it be based on where you are heading and what you dream of accomplishing.

202. Be content with where you are and with what you have, but don't get comfortable and complacent to the point of stagnancy.

203. The art of utilizing wisdom and knowledge: "WISDOM"—not saying everything you know. "KNOWLEDGE" is knowing wisdom is the principal thing when sharing knowledge.

204. Your environment has the potential to suppress your ability or express your creativity.

205. There is a saying that goes, "Opportunity comes knocking at your door." But there are times when it will not come knocking. You need to go seek it out in unpopular places to find the best opportunities.

206. There are various types of inheritance. We have monetary, characteristic, emotional, collateral, and spiritual inheritance. All of these can be good or bad. Choose the best of them to leave for your children and their children.

207. God is not on my shoulder; He is in my life. Therefore, whatever I do is through Him, because of Him, with Him, and by Him. In Him, I live, move and have my being.

208. You can be an eagle by nature but act like a chicken. You can be a racehorse but act like a pony. You can be a cheetah but act like a turtle. It depends on your environment and who is training you.

209. Do not permit anyone to quarantine or confine your feelings. Express yourself and what or how you feel in liberty.

210. Do not put yourself on the 80% sales rack and allow a Chrysler mentality to mistreat your Bentley emotion. Quality and class never go on sale.

211. You are the only one who will invest 100% in yourself 100% of the time.

212. You are "high maintenance," and high maintenance means high standards, integrity, respect, and moral value. To afford you, one MUST have a wealth of these.

213. Change cannot be avoided; it is inevitable. Growth, however, can be altered. Growth is optional; you choose whether to grow.

214. True perfection is never about not failing but about who you are deep within. Perfection is at the core of your heart, making you always seek to do and be better at every opportunity.

215. Make sure you see the value of a thing or person before you invest in it. What you invest could be anything: Your money, your time, your emotion, your energy, and your strength.

216. No matter how brutal, devastating, or dreadful your childhood was, you can still dream big and be successful and happy as an adult.

217. Some people are late starters, and some are late bloomers, but it is not so much about how you start but how you finish that will determine your legacy.

218. I am your friend, but that does not mean you are my friend. I trust myself to be your friend, but I do not trust you to have a friendship with me.

219. As a child, someone else is responsible and must be blamed for everything concerning you. As an adult, you are responsible for everything concerning you. You don't get to blame anyone anymore.

220. Our God listens to us, but we have to listen to our God twice as much.

221. Unmet expectations bring frustration when we expect too many unrealistic things from people who cannot fulfill their own needs and desires. We depend on others to fulfill all our emotional, spiritual, financial, and psychological needs, even when the ones we expect it from are empty and void of these things themselves.

222. One of the most difficult but most necessary things to do is to "wait" on God.

223. We often underestimate our talents and ability until someone points them out to us.

224. Delusions about yourself are a huge roadblock to becoming the best you.

225. Making little progress on one thing is more meaningful than getting nowhere with everything.

226. Your circle can be so huge, yet so small it fits in one hand.

227. The only thing standing between a simple and magnificent you is daily practice.

228. There is a part of each of us that cannot be filled by anything or anyone terrestrial. Only the celestial divinity can reach, touch, and impact that part of us. I want to believe that part is reserved for God.

229. Humanity seeks to fulfill every need and desire according to what they see and feel in nature.

But if they were to reach out and search beyond themselves, they would discover that all needs and desires are met in the heavens where God Almighty dwells, and then are manifested on earth to those who seek it first in the heavenly realm.

230. You have to perceive before you can receive, perception before reception.

231. God does not pay attention to your age; He pays attention to your stage.

232. God did not create you to be weak; He created you to be meek.

233. Satan's devices take away God's advice. But God's advice destroys Satan's devices.

234. Sometimes, to protect your mind, you have to decide not to look behind.

235. Whatever or whoever gets your attention has the ability to control you. That is why Satan's strategy is always to get your attention first.

236. Strength and power without wisdom are recipes for destruction.

237. Women are normally destroyed through or by emotions because we are predominantly emotional beings.

238. Women use sex as a bargaining chip because sex is one thing that most men will do or say anything to get, even if it costs them their position, integrity, money, and even their family.

239. Kings and queens do not chase peasants and paupers.

240. God speaks, but only those who listen will hear, and only those who look will see.

Dear God

Yes, it hurts, and I am hurting. Make me **BETTER** so I won't be bitter.

I **TRUST** you with my life.

Thank you **God**.

@GeorgiaPeterkin

241. Everyone looks, but not everyone sees-Seeing eyes are rare.

242. If only we could see souls more than body, shape, and makeup. How different our idea of beauty would be.

243. There are so many people around you who always need something—your time, your experience, your support, your prayer, your love, your resource. YET, you feel so alone when you need help, time, prayer, love, support, and resources. It is in those moments you truly realize you only have yourself and God to depend on.

244. It is often said, "No pain, no gain." This saying has caused many to accept unnecessary pain, hurt, and hardship, thinking it is the only way to gain, win or achieve. I beg to differ. Not every gain has to be painful. You can win, succeed, and achieve without pain. Life does not always have to be painful to see great results and satisfaction.

245. Nothing hurts a good soul and a kind heart more than living amongst those who see you and treat you as just mere flesh and bones without feelings.

246. Let the pain of your past be your passion for progress.

247. Do not wait until a moment becomes a memory before you value it. Value every moment, those you spend with the ones you love and those you spend by yourself.

248. There is something much deeper and more intense than regular worship or the expensive suit you wear to worship. It is called intimacy. That's a place in worship where you are totally disconnected from your surroundings and drawn into divine reality. This is where you get divine healing and revelation. This is true spirit and soul worship.

249. You can make yourself available to anyone but do not allow yourself to be accessible to everyone.

250. Maturity allows you to think on a higher level than your surroundings, environment, or present circumstances.

251. It is God's responsibility and interest to provide it, but it is our responsibility and interest to reach out and take it.

252. As long as it does not cost you your integrity, soul, and moral values, no price is too high to pay for your dreams and aspirations.

253. Go ahead and dream. Dream of big and ridiculously impossible things. No one else will dream for you. But don't just dream, take the next steps to execute your dreams into reality.

254. Those who took your brightly colored coat and laughed at you will come in shame, asking for forgiveness when they see that even without it, you still dreamed and made it to the top.

255. When you have gathered all your possessions and earned all your achievements, hold them all in your left hand and the word of God in your right hand. Remember, all your blessings come from above, not abroad.

256. Every one of us has a story from before or leading to our success. Embrace it; there's no need to be ashamed of what leads to true success.

257. A queen always maintains her posture. The peasant never sees her distress.

258. I am not an ornament. I am a treasure. Only He who recognizes my value will do what it takes to have me.

259. You cannot manage what you do not control, nor can you teach what you have not mastered.

260. Text messages are nice, but a woman with goals does not build on that. She needs calls, plans, and promises kept.

261. There is no logic in YOU trying to free someone else while YOU are still locked up and locked down.

262. If you must lie, cheat, dim other people's light, and throw others under the bus to get it, then it is not really for you. What is yours comes to you clean and without manipulation.

263. I found out that I am allergic to failure. It does not agree with my mind, body, and spirit. But I also found out that I have an addiction. I am addicted to success, winning, and loving.

264. If you have money but no character, you are still poor. Good character and integrity are universal currency.

265. Gossip is the worst thief. It steals a person's honor, dignity, character, and reputation that many times cannot be restored.

266. When we say we are done, we are tired, but we continue. That's not us, but grace that picks us up where we fail or fall. It's His grace that is sufficient.

267. Intentionally ignore hints so you can speak up and be direct like an adult.

268. My survival mechanism does not have pride. It has integrity, morals, values, good character, and persistence.

269. Ladies, find a man that speaks, and you shut your mouth out of respect for him and not out of fear of him.

270. There is something in each of us for one of us.

271. A hearer hears only words, but a listener hears words, intent, feelings, and even what is said non-verbally.

272. Who am I? I am more than the clothes I wear. I am more than makeup and perfume. I am more than the way I smile. I am more than what you see on the outside. Know me from within, and you will really know WHO I AM.

273. Too blessed to be stressed is a "myth" that many of us believe. Blessed and successful folks have their down days and struggle too.

274. Women, use your charm to IMPACT men, not to attract them.

275. God is sovereign; He breaks every rule to accomplish His will. He is not subjected to systems or

regulations. He goes beyond barriers and gets the job done.

276. Some will reject the truth just because it is coming from you. That's not your problem; let the truth be told anyway.

277. If there is absolutely nothing in you that someone can copy or be encouraged by, then you are living a meaningless life.

278. There is no such thing as "Saved and Sexy." Sexy is for your spouse, and saved is for your soul. You need to be an impacting and attracting Christian. Impacting lives positively and attracting people with your lifestyle and attitude will lead them to salvation.

279. Your problems, failures, or weaknesses are not unique, but YOU are unique.

280. You can edit your life story as often as you like. It is yours to do, not anyone else's. But know that whatever changes you make come with consequences.

281. If you are undecided, you have still decided. You have decided to be undecided.

282. Find the good and highlight it; see the bad and correct it.

283. In every situation, good or bad, look at yourself and see how you have contributed to it.

284. What a pity it would be if you were only useful to yourself. It would be a total waste of so many possibilities.

285. Just because a person has class or elegance doesn't mean they are proud-spirited. You can indeed be classy, elegant, suave, and yet full of humility.

286. Be careful not to just exist in life instead of living life.

287. Do not assume responsibility for a person's misconception or preconception of you.

288. A closed door does not mean a locked door. A locked door needs a key; a closed door needs only

the knob to turn. Understand the difference in your pursuit of opportunities.

289. Saying goodbye does not require the approval of the person you are saying goodbye to.

290. The person who will make you feel guilty for making a good decision is never someone you need during your growth process.

291. Truth should be the foundation of every relationship, but some relationships are built on lies and deception.

292. Life, time, and energy are too valuable to be wasted on dead-end conversations. Don't go down that road.

293. It is easy to be wise when looking into someone else's life, but wisdom becomes a stranger to you in your own life.

294. Anger produces and sends out the most hurtful and painful words that cannot be recalled or taken off the heart's shelf by rationality and excuses.

295. Be with someone that will keep your secret, not someone that can only keep you a secret.

296. Do not mistake disrespect for honesty. Being "brutally honest" means telling the truth without sugarcoating it. Being disrespectful means not paying attention to how you speak and bringing forth your truth or the words you use.

297. People grow when they are loved well. If you truly want to help someone heal, grow, and become better, love them well. Love them totally without any agenda. Love them without any reason to love them, love them when they are difficult to love, and love them even when they reject the love. Love them back to life.

298. We must learn what we expect. If you expect to get married, learn about marriage. If you expect to have a business, learn about business management. If you expect honesty and respect, learn to show respect and be honest. If you want to get into ministry, learn Biblical principles.

299. Sometimes, jealousy isn't only about what you have materially. People envy the way you speak,

the way you walk, the way you carry yourself. Some people are even jealous of how you survived problems that everyone thought would have destroyed you, but you went through them and came out whole, and that breeds jealousy because they expected you to break or even die.

300. Some people are just not worth seeing your tears. Let them wonder if you are hurting.

LUKE 12:15

Then he said to them. "**Watch out!** Be on your **GUARD** against all kinds of **greed**; life does not consist in an **ABUNDANCE** of **possessions.**"

@GeorgiaPeterkin

301. Surround yourself with people you would not mind trading places with; you cannot allow a broke person to tell you how to make money or someone who constantly lives on welfare to tell you how to be independent.

302. Sometimes, it is profitable to act as if you don't know or understand, even if you do. This allows you to learn a new way and understand how others do things and think. Everyone has their method, and it's ok to learn them all.

303. Your personal belief does not constitute the written Holy Word of God. Do not preach your belief; preach the gospel.

304. A beautiful heart that is sincere and pure is seen in the character of a person. It is the ability not to hold grudges and not to consider wrongs done to you when it is time for you to be kind.

305. Giving up all you want, at times, is what is needed to have everything you need.

306. Excuses are easier to make than decisions by people without emotional strength, psychological motivation, and awareness.

307. There are times when everything becomes too much. Too much pain, too much hurt, too much failure, too many broken promises and shattered dreams, too many fake friends, too many disloyal family members, too much deception and lies, too much to do, too weak, too tired, too depressed, too broke, too confused. With all those things that are "TOO MUCH," believe that this TOO shall pass. And it's never too much for God to handle.

308. Some people get so addicted to trash that even when they have treasure, they treat it the same as they do trash.

309. When a woman has the right man, submission becomes automatic and with pleasure.

310. It's amazing how the PhD. of a woman can be led by the GED of a man when she's in love.

311. Women can allow themselves to be so blinded by love that they cannot see that the man leading them is going nowhere.

312. Don't be so desperate for a man that you settle for a boy with a beard.

313. God's plan is better than our dreams; God's purpose is better than what we wish. Allow yourself to yield to the will of God and what He has in store for you.

314. You can fight everything, but you cannot fight love. You can ignore and deny it, but you just cannot fight love. Love is stronger than you; love is powerful, and love does not give up and go away. You have to surrender to the power of love.

315. Do not try to resuscitate what is dead and should remain dead in your life.

316. Get rid of the expired things in your life—expired people, expired emotions, expired attitudes, and expired expectations. If not, they will poison you mentally, emotionally, and characteristically

because you have allowed yourself to consume expired things and people.

317. Excellence is what sets you apart. "RARE" is what puts you in demand.

318. They say a picture is worth a thousand words. Though it might be worth a thousand words, it could be a thousand false words. Sometimes, pictures do lie. Even more, when they are old pictures, resurrected in an attempt to re-live the past. I advise you: Be up-to-date, live up to date. Many lives are lived in masks and make-believe, as a result, people fool others and fool themselves.

319. Get in the habit of lending someone a helping hand before you ask someone to give you a hand.

320. From afar, things can look beautiful and real, but you can see so many impurities, imperfections, and flaws up close. People are the same.

321. Look where others won't so you can see what others can't. Go where no one else has gone so you can be the trailblazer of that path.

322. There are some relationships that belong in the realm of where you are coming from and not in the realm of where you are going.

323. When you stop blaming others, even if they are to be blamed, you will start taking responsibility for your past, present, and future.

324. The people you accommodate and the crowd you entertain regularly will determine where you are going and what you'll achieve. As the saying goes, "Run with wolves, and you will learn how to howl. Fly with eagles, and you will learn how to soar."

325. Do not let ignorance challenge your intelligence.

326. To wrestle with the ignorant requires you to operate from the realm where you have wisdom, control, and intelligence. There is no way they will allow you to lower yourself to a level of ignorance.

327. In matters of conversation or debate, let others step up to your level. If you move from where you are, let it be to a higher intellect.

328. If you are a strong opponent, then players will not approach you carelessly because they know you will always read their game before they start to play with or around you.

329. Do not give audience to strong-armed, weak-hearted men; they only have muscular strength and arrogance to show.

330. Favor and faith are two lethal components of victory.

331. Aim long enough for one of your bullets to hit multiple targets, and plan and strategize carefully before executing.

332. When you know that you know what you need to know, that's all you need to know.

333. Say nothing. Saying "NOTHING" can be your secret to achieving many things.

334. A process without progress is useless.

335. Motivational words are never to be taken for the gospel. Motivational speech cannot replace the Holy Word of God.

336. If someone points out your sin or your wrongs, they are not judging you. They are making you aware of your errors.

337. Do not suppress your feelings, whatever they are. Suppressed feelings will poison you internally; express them responsibly.

338. When arrogance and ignorance come knocking, let wisdom answer. Only wisdom knows how to respond to them.

339. To have victory, I must not be afraid to engage in battle with whoever or whatever opposes me.

340. When you fight against the hand of God, you will never win. When you fight with the hands of God, victory is sure.

341. God gets all the glory; it is His anyway, but He ensures victory is mine.

342. When you are sure it is God who calls you, justifies you, redeems you, and sets you apart for good works, you do not pay attention to all those who have their jealous eyes and negative words to say about you.

343. God is the ultimate and the infinite. He is the one that justifies and vindicates. No one can reverse God's good or bad judgment on any matter; He overrules and overturns every other judgment and decision of man.

344. I speak to your heart, not your emotion. What is spoken to emotions disappears when the emotion subsides, but what is spoken to the heart remains long after it has been said.

345. The way I am feeling is like angels are hustling about in a frenzy, getting busy in a hurry, JUST FOR ME. I know God remembered me the way He remembered Hannah or Noah.

346. Keep getting up; one day, you will walk away from it and leave them all behind—all that is causing you to fall.

347. Sometimes in true friendship, no matter how much it hurts, you just have to allow people to walk through their storms alone and pray they make it through. Just be prepared to be that rainbow they seek after the storm has passed. No questions, no judgment, no worries. We must remember everything isn't about us. Some journeys are personal ones. Stay focused on your journey but be ready to help another on theirs when the time comes. Remember, you can't control someone else's destiny, it's hard enough trying to manage your own, but you sure can be at the finish line waiting for them with open arms and a smile.

348. If you stop finding fault in the man, you will see he is not as bad as you say he is. He just needs to be respected.

349. Peace, love, happiness, comfort, stability, joy, and laughter are all part of marriage. Living without those primary things makes no sense just to say, "So you are married."

350. Nowadays, women are dating "down," and men are marrying "up." That means women marry out of desperation, and men marry for security—

both are wrong. Whatever happened to eating alone until someone comes along, not just to eat with you but also to bring something of substance to your table? Where are the men who know and understand their role as the "primary provider" even if the woman is financially stable? Why can't women realize they are worth more than settling for a non-progressive element in the form of a man just because he looks good or has a mouth full of sweet nothings? Listen, there are still great responsible men out there, and there are still great respectful women out there that will do right by you. Quit being an opportunist and quit settling for less than you deserve.

351.   The truth punches below the belt but lies break the heart. Deception blinds the eyes, but reality hits you in the face. These fights can be avoided if we accept what our head tells us. Our brain is speaking, but the heart is not listening.

352.   Today is a good day; today is a blessed day. All is well, and if all is not well, it WILL be well. The rain is good, the sun is good, and the snow is good. I am equipped to deal with whatever the day is. I am equipped to deal with whatever life offers—

challenging days and situations, favorable days and opportunities. I get tired sometimes, and that's okay. I rest when I am tired. I get frustrated sometimes, and that is also okay. I take a deep breath, allowing myself to realize that I am still breathing, which means I am still in the game. During my times of frustration, I do what I feel like doing at that time, even if it is nothing. I allow my tears to flow freely so that my inner self can be relaxed and released. I do not look for pity; I seek opportunities. I do not complain, but I voice my concerns. I AM CONFIDENT IN WHO I AM IN CHRIST, and that makes everything just right.

353. It is wise to take lessons from certain animal instincts; they are always alert to their surroundings. Nothing or no one creeps up on them unaware.

354. Let God arise, and his enemies be scattered. Let everyone that believes in the Lord take confidence in that when God arises, all our enemies will be scattered like the dry leaves that the wind drives away.

355. Some of us are INDISPENSABLE. But only a few of us are irreplaceable.

356. Shakespeare wrote: "The meaning of life is to find your gift. The purpose of life is to give it away." When you find your gift, do not hide it under a bushel because you think it's less valuable than someone else's or because someone rejected it when you offered it. Believe that someone is out there eagerly waiting to accept your gift with open arms and a heart filled with gratitude. Find your gift and share it with whoever needs it, there are many who do.

357. God is the vindicator of the pure in heart and clean hands. Stand still and you will see.

358. Do not strive to be someone people need. Be someone that people appreciate and respect. People can hate and abuse and mishandle what they need. But they will never hate or abuse what or who they appreciate and respect.

359. You will understand it someday. Not everything God does in our lives is meant for us to understand. Sometimes, life doesn't make sense

at all, and that's just fine. God is not obligated to explain every single detail, every why, when, where, and how to us. In fact, our wisdom might complicate things, seeing that the ALL-WISE God's foolishness surpasses our most intellectual wisdom. What God is doing in your life right now is not meant to be understood or explained just yet.

360. Put your faith in action and allow God to do what is necessary. Allow God to stir up your nest, to shake up your present life so He can reposition you for the future He has in store for you. God sees things you cannot see right now, which will prevent you from prospering in the future. He sees the pitfalls, holes, plots, snares, and everything you are blinded to. Things may not make any sense to you right now, but trust the process, trust God. In His perfect timing, all will be revealed to you. God will open your eyes when everything is in place and lined up for your smooth transition into your planned future of hope, peace, joy, prosperity, and love. You will see why you were going through so much, why people turned against you, why you were rejected, and why people left you. All the puzzle pieces will be put together and converge

into a meaningful design. But for now, trust God. "Be still and know that He is GOD." Psalm 46:10

361. A useful and helpful woman is precious in the life of any man. Such a woman makes a man feel like he has an awesome gift from God that he must cherish. By appreciating and caring for your gift, you bring honor to the giver (GOD) and raise your value among men.

362. Ladies, it is good that you want him to find you stunning and beautiful. But what you really need is for him to find you "irreplaceable."

363. Good SEX blinds you to the truth about a person. A good partner opens your eyes to a person. Good SEX comes around to be satisfied; a good partner sees that your needs are met, and you are satisfied. Good SEX holds sex and other things against you; a good partner ensures nothing comes against you.

364. The presence of God is where we are strongest. Everything there is done in the strength of God. And every fight is a FIXED fight, where you are set to win.

" Because we are
flawed humans, it is
INEVITABLE that
we will cause **HARM**
and **disappointment**
to others,
INADVERTENTLY or
otherwise.

@GeorgiaPeterkin

WHAT I TELL MYSELF

_____

_____

_____

_____

_____

_____

_____

_____

_____

_____

WHAT I TELL MYSELF

_____

_____

_____

_____

_____

_____

_____

_____

_____

_____

WHAT I TELL MYSELF

_____

_____

_____

_____

_____

_____

_____

_____

_____

_____

_____

WHAT I TELL MYSELF

_____

_____

_____

_____

_____

_____

_____

_____

_____

_____

_____

WHAT I TELL MYSELF

_____

_____

_____

_____

_____

_____

_____

_____

_____

_____